# KOTAN CHRONICLES

# Kotan Chronicles

## Selected Poems 1928–1943

Genzō Sarashina

*Translated by Nadine Willems*

ISOBAR
PRESS

First published in 2017 by

Isobar Press
Sakura 2-21-23-202, Setagaya-ku,
Tokyo 156-0053, Japan
&
14 Isokon Flats, Lawn Road,
London NW3 2XD, United Kingdom

http://isobarpress.com

ISBN 978-4-907359-19-5 (paperback)
ISBN 978-4-907359-20-1 (hardback)



Acknowledgements

Some of these translations were first published in *Cha: An Asian Literary Journal.* Cover photograph: 'Ainu Village' by Leonard Halford Dudley Buxton (2004.135.1.227) copyright © Pitt-Rivers Museum, University of Oxford. Back-cover photograph of Genzō Sarashina with Ainu companions courtesy of Richard Siddle; photographs of Kussharo Kotan Elementary School and Teshikaga courtesy of Teshikaga Town Library; map of north-eastern Hokkaido by Jon Gregory; photograph of Lake Mashū by Nadine Willems.

## Contents


*Preface* 9
*Introduction* 13
*Translator's Note* 33

FROM *Seed Potatoes* (1930)

*As the Old Man Told Me* 37
Bear Story 39
Blizzard in the Kotan 41
Isn't It So? 43
Kotan Chronicle 45
Scum Town 47
The Mad Entomologist 49
Kei and Potatoes 51
The Substitute Teacher's Poem 52
Small Footprints 55
Poverty and Autumn Rain 56
Salmon 58
Snowstorm 59

POEMS FROM THE EARLY 1930S

Kotan School Poems 63

*Poem for Sekko* 63
*Make-Believe Work* 65
*Constellations* 66
*Mamo's Poem* 67

*Attendance Rate* 69
*The Absentee* 70
*Geographical Offence* 71
*The Meaning of 'Barbarian'* 72
*Summer* 73

*Graduation Ceremony* 74

National Census 75
Leaving the Kotan 83

FROM *Songs of the Frozen Plain* (1943)

Forest 89
Lake Mashū 92
Angry Okhotsk 93
Cranes 94
The Grey Heron 95
Kuccharo Kotan 96

*Notes on the poems* 99

*Ainu glossary* 104
*Japanese glossary* 105

## List of Illustrations

Map of north-eastern Hokkaido 12
The town of Teshikaga *circa* 1930 36
Kussharo Kotan Elementary School in 1939 62
Lake Mashū 88

## Cover Photograph

*Kotan* is the Ainu word for village. The photograph on the cover, taken by the British anthropologist Leonard Halford Dudley Buxton (1890–1939) and first published in 1924 in his book *The Eastern Road*, shows an Ainu village in Hokkaido in 1922.

*Throughout the book Japanese names appear with the surname first, except for Sarashina's name on the cover and title page, and in citations in the notes of Japanese authors who publish primarily in English.*

# Preface

I discovered the work of Sarashina Genzō by pure chance. I was researching the history of intellectual exchanges between European and Japanese radicals in the pre-war period, when in a city library I came across several poetry magazines to which he had contributed. These mimeographed magazines had been published in Kushiro, eastern Hokkaido, in the early 1930s.

I found the poems intriguing as they varied so much in style and subject matter. They conveyed feelings of empathy for fellow human beings and awe for the natural world, but with little sentimentality. They described everyday life with lucidity and a rare lightness of touch. As it turned out, Sarashina became well-known in his native Hokkaido, but he never reached a large audience in the rest of Japan and has never been translated into English or any other language in spite of having written about such essential themes as the encounter between Japanese and the indigenous Ainu, and the socio-political transformation of Hokkaido that took place at the time.

The poems selected for the present volume illustrate these themes and reflect the particular quality of Sarashina's style. They represent a small fraction of his total output, and only include poems written up to the early 1940s. The texts not only constitute an interesting source for the historian, but they are also rich from a literary perspective. The blending of voices, and often languages, that runs through them creates a real singularity of expression. Sarashina's poetry has long deserved to be known outside of Japan. This book is a small step to making that happen.

A translation project like this one is not a solo enterprise. It relies on the assistance of many people and institutions. My heartfelt gratitude goes in the first instance to the Daiwa Anglo-Japanese Foundation whose generosity made possible a trip to Hokkaido in the spring of 2016. Exploring the physical and cultural landscapes where the poems of this volume were written was an essential and eye-opening part of the work.

Paul Rossiter, the founder of Isobar Press and a poet in his own right, put a great deal of trust and commitment into this project right from its early beginnings. It would never have reached completion without his patience, guidance and dedication. His help with the phrasing of the translations and the finding of an English 'voice' for Sarashina has been indispensable.

Various people have shared their expertise – linguistic or other – at various stages of the project. I am especially thankful to Murai Mayako, whose careful and perceptive reading of the texts contributed to the overall clarity of the translation. Professors Katō Hirofumi and Tangiku Itsuji, from the Hokkaido University Center for Indigenous and Ainu Studies, offered help and encouragement when I first started researching Sarashina's poetry. Makihara Daisuke, from Teshikaga Town Library, was a particularly valuable guide to the Sarashina Genzō archives.

I am indebted to Soga Eiko, whose artistic sensibility and understanding of Ainu culture have been inspiring all along.

I am also grateful for the contributions of Richard Siddle, Jeffry Gayman, Sarashina Kō and Jon Gregory; of the staff at the Bodleian Japanese Library in Oxford, at the Sapporo Prefectural Museum of Literature, and at the Tenjinyama Studio in Sapporo; and of Professor Itō Shigeyuki and Peter Tasker.

Despite the generous help received from so many people, mistakes may remain, and, as customary, I take full responsibility for every single one of them.

North-eastern Hokkaido

# Introduction

Hokkaido is known today as one of the four major islands that, together with thousands of smaller islands, make up the Japanese archipelago. Its capital, Sapporo, is a bustling modern city with a population of close to two million. Yet in the early Meiji period (1868–1912), the northern island was thought of as a *terra nullius* available to be settled, developed and modernized. The invisibility of the Ainu in early-Meiji Japan extended to the world of literature, where writers commonly referred to it as a barren wilderness that bore no trace of human life.[1]

In reality the Ainu Moshir – literally 'the great calm land where Ainu reside' – which encompassed present-day Hokkaido, Sakhalin, the Kuril Islands, parts of Honshu, the southern Kamchatka peninsula and the region of the Amur River estuary, had been inhabited by Ainu people for centuries before its incorporation into modern national entities.

It was not until the 1920s that the Ainu finally found visibility and a voice in the Japanese literary landscape, notably in the work of Hokuto Iboshi (1902–1929). A poet of Ainu lineage whose family had adopted a Japanese name, he was a passionate supporter of Ainu identity. The work of some fully Japanese writers also displayed a strong sense of empathy with the region's indigenous peoples, questioning on their behalf the rationale of subjugation set out by the national government. An example is 'The Flying Sled', a long poem about the encounter in Sakhalin of a larger-than-life Ainu man and a Japanese ranger, written by Oguma Hideo (1901–1940) in the mid-1930s.

The poems assembled in this volume similarly address the plight of the Ainu in the context of Japanese development of the island, but in a far from straightforward manner. Sarashina Genzō was himself a second-generation settler and participated in the settlers' experience of poverty, struggle, hope and despair. In describing seemingly innocuous events and encounters, he weaves an intricate pattern of life in eastern Hokkaido in the 1920s and 1930s, a world where Ainu and Japanese shared the experience of disturbance and transformation, and where the overwhelming power of nature provided the backdrop for a clash of cultures replete with contradictions. The poems are also a reminder of the diversity of proletarian literature in the period. Enriched by transnational links, Sarashina's work was part of a larger anti-establishment movement that rejected Marxist theory in favour of non-violent anarchism. Its supporters espoused a form of egalitarian and humanistic politics that censorship, repression and war would soon sweep away together with all other forms of dissent.

Sarashina was born in January 1904 in the town of Teshikaga on the eastern side of Hokkaido. He was the son of Sarashina Jirō and Yori, first generation settlers who had migrated from Niigata Prefecture in the late 1880s. In the face of poverty and a hostile climate, the family started cultivating potatoes, soybeans and cereals, later moving into dairy farming. Teshikaga is located at the edge of a vast plain, halfway between the port of Kushiro on the Pacific Ocean to the south and the Okhotsk Sea to the north. From rudimentary beginnings, the town had gradually developed along a bend of the Kushiro River, forced labour by prisoners providing half of the man-power necessary for building its infrastructure and working the nearby sulphur mine.[2] At the time of Sarashina's birth, it was still a disorderly collection of wooden structures, crisscrossed by muddy roads and regularly engulfed in thick layers of the mist typical of the area.

Access to the town remained difficult and fog frequently jeopardized agricultural work, yet the area was prized for the stark beauty of its mountains and lakes. A few miles to the north-east is Lake Mashū. A well-frequented tourist spot today, it is a deep, transparent-blue caldera lake that has long inspired Ainu mythology. Further to the west, Lake Kussharo lies between forest and mountains. In the early days of settlement, a dozen Ainu dwellings formed the Kussharo *kotan* on the shore. In the early

1900s, it grew to about twenty households after a government-ordained merger with another village. Although imposed on unequal terms, the interaction between Ainu and *wajin*, the Japanese migrant settlers, proved mostly peaceful and quickly shaped the fabric of everyday life. From the Ainu, Japanese migrants learnt how to cope with long and harsh winters; for example, they increasingly relied on slow-burning elm wood to keep fires alive.[3] Sarashina Genzō grew up in this environment shaped by the drudgery of agricultural work, the proximity of Ainu culture, and the majestic scenery of eastern Hokkaido.

In 1921, the young Sarashina enrolled in veterinary school in Tokyo in order to acquire skills useful in animal husbandry. His first tentative poem was produced back in Hokkaido during the summer vacation, when he was moved by the sight of flowers on the grave of his older sister Miyo, who had died in infancy. However, ill health and the Great Kanto Earthquake of 1923 forced him to withdraw from school after just two years and return to Hokkaido for good. During his time in Tokyo he had mingled with left-leaning intellectuals and literati, such as agrarian thinker Eto Tekirei (1880–1944) and poet Ozaki Kihachi (1892–1974), and after his return to Hokkaido he maintained these contacts, winning fourth prize as a newcomer given by the journal *Jojōshi* (Lyric Poetry) in 1925. Gradually he devoted more energy to literary production, contributing to and editing poetry magazines while living off meagre financial means. With many other settlers in Hokkaido in the pre-war period, he shared the risk of destitution and serious illness.

## POETRY OF DISSENT

By the late 1920s, Sarashina had abandoned pure lyricism in favour of a form of poetry that was socially and politically engaged. He belonged to a group of poet-activists based around Kushiro who remained in regular contact with intellectuals in the rest of the country. They all believed that their literary medium had transformative social potential and sided with those they saw as beleaguered victims of modernization and capitalist development, including outcastes and colonized subjects. In this respect, they were part of the wave of proletarian literature that was at its strongest in Japan in the mid-1920s and early 1930s.[4]

Spurred by the advent of the Bolshevik revolution and encouraged by an international network of left-wing literary circles, proletarian writers emphasized solidarity with the underclass and the need to stand up to oppression. The work and tragic death in prison of Kobayashi Takiji (1903–1933) best represent the movement's thwarted ambitions. Himself a resident of Hokkaido, Kobayashi is particularly known for the publication in 1929 of *Kani kōsen* (The Crab-Cannery Ship), a short novel that described the horrific working conditions in a fishing boat off the coast of Kamchatka and the crew's mutiny and doomed take-over of the craft. The author's overt communist leanings effectively signed his death warrant. He died in February 1933 after torture and severe beatings in police custody.[5]

Sarashina and his circle shared with proletarian writers a critique of capitalist society and a belief in the need for resistance. They forged intellectual connections in the literary cliques and publications of proletarian militants, but their work was distinctive and recognized as such by their contemporaries. In their view, the real enemy was authoritarianism, indeed any limitation of human freedom, whether imposed by the Japanese government or by Marxist ideologues. They were thus highly critical of the authoritarian turn taken in Russia by Bolshevism in government and avoided the strident calls for class struggle of many Japanese proletarian writers of the period.[6] As Sarashina's work demonstrates so well, they remained sharp and sympathetic observers of the everyday life of the lower strata of the population in all its mundanity and desperation. The focus was less on engineering an ideal future society than on the expression of real life struggles in a changing and unfair world.[7]

The particular environment of eastern Hokkaido further shaped Sarashina's poetic voice. The region's development depended to a large extent on farming activities, which provided another source of literary inspiration. It is no surprise that he named his first poetry collection, published in 1930, *Taneimo* (Seed Potatoes). The image in his poem 'Kei and Potatoes' of a farmer's child staggering under the weight of a sack of seed potatoes while the farmer himself hopes, against the odds, for a plentiful harvest fittingly illustrates the challenges faced by migrant settlers at the time. As a participant-observer, Sarashina was more in tune with farmers' concerns than those of the urban proletariat. In that sense, he was a 'poet of the soil'. Unlike several of his contemporaries, however, he did not idealize cultivation of the land. His poetry communicates the hardships and dangers of the farmers' lives and questions the system that allowed such precariousness to persist. While Sarashina was not directly involved in the growing labour movement, he is credited with having played a pioneering role in the area's literary scene as an engaged *nōmin shijin* (farmer-poet).[8]

Like the rest of Japan, Hokkaido in the late 1920s and 1930s suffered from economic and political instability. The Showa Depression of 1930–31 that followed the financial crash of 1929 markedly affected employment and living standards. In the countryside the years between 1930 and 1934 proved especially challenging. A sharp drop in agricultural prices constituted the main reason for reduced incomes. Lack of jobs in the cities also resulted in a higher number of mouths to feed in rural areas, either because out-of-work urban labourers were encouraged to return home or because of a slowdown in the migration of labour to the cities.[9]

As some poems make painfully clear, during the early 1930s hunger and scarcity were common occurrences in farming communities. Damage inflicted on crops by adverse weather compounded the effect of the economic downturn, especially in northern prefectures.[10] Reports in 1931 talked of children unable to bring a lunchbox to school and people forced to eat oats intended as horse fodder.[11] Moreover, tensions in the farming sector were rife, as a growing number of cultivators, in part motivated by left-wing ideas, contested the terms of their tenancy agreements with landlords.

By the late 1920s, censorship and repression had regained harshness after several years of relative leniency. The government targeted radical dissent, especially in the form of communist and anarchist ideas, which it saw as a threat to public order. The imprisonment of hundreds of left-wing activists in March 1928 marked a decisive moment in this programme of repression. Japan's escalating aggression in China and an increasingly authoritarian regime at home would follow in the 1930s.

Early in 1936, the Tokkō, the 'Thought Police', detained Sarashina for interrogation because of alleged links to the 'Kokushoku Gang' incident, an occurrence of anarchist agitation by a group of rural youths based in Nagano prefecture. The group, intent on alleviating poverty in the countryside, had increasingly resorted to violent action to achieve its objectives, including an attempted bank robbery in Tokyo in November 1935. The police suspected that another plot was in preparation and that Sarashina might be hiding a fugitive and so took the poet in for questioning.

As it turned out, he was released the next day after a local businessman interceded on his behalf.[12] Although Sarashina had made his political allegiance clear in the past – as when he forged connections with anarchist-leaning activists in the mid-1920s and acted as representative of the Nōmin Jichikai (Farmers' Self-Governing Council) for Hokkaido – the risk of opposing the country's official ideology, even by peaceful means, had become less and less of an option. Sarashina's detainment for questioning was evidence of enhanced pressure on dissidents.

In the publishing sector, the constant menace of police suppression resulted in self-censorship by authors and editors. Sarashina's use of *fuseji* – circles or crosses replacing 'dangerous' words in sentences – indicates that like many others he could not ignore the politically stifling atmosphere of the era.[13] And while it was left to readers to guess the author's intentions, in general they needed little imagination. The law had made clear that criticism of the imperial system or the principle of private property would attract stiff punishment.[14]

In the eastern corner of Hokkaido some fresh literary endeavours thrived nevertheless, perhaps due to a sense of urgency in such volatile times. The launch in January 1930 of the journal *Hokui gojūdo* (Latitude Fifty Degrees North) confirmed Sarashina's position in the region's poetic landscape. This mimeographed periodical, which he edited with poet and local historian Watanabe Shigeru (1907–1982), ran for a total of twelve issues until 1935. *Hokui gojūdo*'s distinctive character was the outcome of its unusual mosaic of contributors and the vision of the world they conveyed. As editor, Sarashina could count on several of his friends who actively tilled the land, such as farmer-poets Igari Mitsunao (1898–1938) and Makabe Jin (1907–1984), and his own wife Hanako, whom he married in 1931. All shared the experience of trying to make a living on the rough plains of northern Japan. But the periodical effectively had a nationwide reach. Several contributors, such as famed writer and sculptor Takamura Kōtaro (1883–1956), lived in Tokyo, and a few others hailed from distant prefectures.

The common thread of their work was simple, almost naïve. It conveyed a heightened sensitivity to the natural world coupled with a feeling of indebtedness toward it. For these poets, it was crucial to recognize that human beings amounted to very little on their own, but belonged to a wider web of connectedness woven by nature. This acknowledgement required humility and a constantly renewed sense of wonder towards the natural environment. It also inspired empathy toward fellow humans. The handful of Japanese scholars who have looked at *Hokui gojūdo* stress the 'humanistic' undercurrents that ran through its pages, although its texts were also imbued with a spirit of rebellion.[15] Implied was adherence to the anarchist conception of 'mutual aid', which, in the poets' view, provided the best alternative to Bolshevist social control by force. In traditional anarchist thought, man is free to choose cooperation over competition. For *Hokui gojūdo*'s poets, extolling the virtues of symbiosis within nature in its broadest sense was another way of celebrating individual freedom.

It is no surprise then to find among *Hokui gojūdo*'s contributors Kusano Shinpei (1903–1988), whose 1928 collection of poems, *The Hundredth Class*, uncannily allows frogs to question the exalted status of their fellow creatures, human beings.[16] Likewise, another of *Hokui gojūdo*'s contributors was Nakanishi Godō (1895–1985), an ornithologist, a close observer of symbiotic relationships between living organisms, and a pioneer of Japan's environmental movement. In the minds of these thinkers, consideration of the natural world led to lessons worth learning for the management of human affairs. Sarashina went to the length of writing a poem ('The Mad Entomologist') about French entomologist Jean-Henri Fabre (1823–1915) precisely in order to express this concern. This engagement with Fabre confirms his closeness to anarchist thinkers, who in the 1920s were the main disseminators of Fabre's series of *Souvenirs entomologiques*, which they translated under the title *Konchūki*.[17] In line with Fabre's own doubts, the poem muses about the meaning of Darwin's evolutionary theory and rejects its embrace of competition as the exclusive directing principle of life, an issue also addressed in Sarashina's 'Salmon' and other poems concerned with the theme of survival of the fittest.

The belief in human agency also influenced poetic form. If men and women were to be free, they had to liberate themselves from restrictive literary rules, such as those of classical Japanese poetry. In place of the formalism of haiku and tanka, Japanese modernists chose free verse and novel imagery and turned to the West for inspiration. Sarashina's literary circle followed a similar approach, but the western non-conformist poetics they sought to emulate belonged in many cases specifically to socially conscious writers like themselves. Takamura Kōtaro greatly admired the Belgian symbolist Emile Verhaeren (1855–1916), and his translations of Verhaeren's work circulated among his friends in the north, while the literary magazine *Shijōritsu* (Supreme Law), to which Sarashina contributed, and which was a direct precursor of *Hokui gojūdo*, ran several issues featuring the Belgian poet. Verhaeren's preoccupation with social justice mirrored that of Hokkaido's farmer-poets. The title *Hokui gojūdo* implied that Japan's new culture would emerge from barren lands at or near latitude fifty degrees north.[18] That geographical line, which runs through both Belgium and Sakhalin Island to the north of Hokkaido, also evoked the transnational imagination that fuelled Japanese literary activities at the time.

## AINU MOSHIR

The word *Ainu* means 'human', so Ainu Moshir means 'the land of humans'. Life amongst the ancestral inhabitants of this land had a decisive effect on both Sarashina's view of the world and his poetry. He had been mingling with them since childhood, as his house in Teshikaga served as a way station for Ainu people walking through the snow between their *kotan* (village) and the city of Kushiro.[19] He became fascinated by their culture and stories and increasingly curious about indigenous conceptions of the natural world. At twenty-two years old, he dedicated one of his poems, 'Taiyōka' (Sunflowers), to the Ainu. Perhaps for him life in a *kotan* conjured up the anarchist ideal of a harmonious community,[20] and certainly Ainu culture's holistic understanding of the natural environment fits into an anarchist worldview. His poetry of the time conveys a real sense of closeness to Ainu people and an awed appreciation of the richness of their world.

Ainu culture is shamanistic. Ainu Moshir exists in harmony with Kamui Moshir, the spirit world. The close connection between people and nature mirrors the connection that exists between the physical and intangible worlds. As in other shamanistic societies, the Ainu revere god-spirits and celebrate religious rituals aimed at maintaining a balanced relationship between the two realms.

God-spirits are thought to visit the land of humans in the form of flora, fauna, natural phenomena, and implements related to daily life. Amongst the most highly respected of these god-spirits – as can be seen by the grandmother's actions in part 4 of Sarashina's poem 'National Census' – is the goddess of fire, or the hearth deity (Abe-kamui, or Kamui-huchi), because of her vital function in the home. Animals such as owls and bears also occupy a special status. The Ainu believe that god-spirits take the shape of animals in order to provide meat and fur (or skin) for human consumption. In return for the privilege of hunting them in their earthly form, humans are expected to conduct prayers, offerings and ceremonies that facilitate the passage of the god-spirits back to Kamui Moshir.

Sarashina's mention in his poem 'Blizzard in the Kotan' of bear blood spilled on the snow refers to *iomande*, an important bear 'sending-off' ceremony. It consisted of the ritual killing of a two-year old cub taken from its mother in infancy and raised as a guest in the *kotan* until the day of its sacrifice. The practice was very elaborate and demanded long preparation. To Sarashina, this intriguing and powerful symbolism also pointed to the plight of a people who found it difficult to confront the modern world because of deeply held beliefs.

Although critical at times, Sarashina cultivated deep bonds of affection for Ainu people. In that respect, his experience as a teacher in a primary school near Kussharo Lake in 1930–31 was transformative. He developed an emotional attachment to the school's seventeen pupils, most of them Ainu. It was from these children and other residents of the *kotan* that he derived many of the stories he transposed into poems. Ainu children were often hungry, as were the children of Japanese settlers (whom

Sarashina had also briefly taught in 1929 in Kumaushi Shōei Primary School in Teshikaga, an experience reflected in his 'The Substitute Teacher's Poem'). But whether Japanese or Ainu, all these children possessed the same capacity for wonder and growth. They marvelled at the night's bright constellations or at seeing for the first time a train running on the newly opened line between Kushiro and Teshikaga. Some fished in the river to put food on the family table. Others were left all day to fend for themselves while their parents worked miles away for logging companies or as farm-hands.

As a teacher, Sarashina had mixed feelings about the system of Ainu education. He was vocal about what he saw as the absurdity of the Japanese government's policy of assimilating Hokkaido's indigenous population.[21] From its initial annexation of Ezo, soon to be renamed Hokkaido, in 1869, the Meiji state aimed to refashion the Ainu people into imperial subjects. That meant a forced and systematic process of acculturation engineered by the government. Early assimilation measures included assigning Japanese names to Ainu families, banning customs such as tattooing for women and ear-piercing for men, and prohibiting other rituals that carried special meaning in Ainu folklore.

The enactment of the Former Natives Protection Law of 1899 further tightened assimilation. In the minds of the Meiji rulers, the development of Hokkaido required the Ainu to convert to regulated farming, and this law created an official framework for the establishment of Ainu agricultural communities. Land endowment was supposed to allow integration into the Japanese population. In practice, however, this legal framework restricted Ainu freedom of movement and action, while confirming their unequal status. Critics have suggested that the 1899 law, even though ostensibly aimed at the protection of Hokkaido's indigenous population, ensured the persistence of discrimination by labelling the Ainu 'former natives'. It denied Ainu their ethnic identity while not considering them fully Japanese.[22]

The integration of Ainu communities into the Japanese state

also meant the continued erosion of traditional practices. Restrictions on deer hunting and salmon and trout catching, in place even before the law of 1899, disrupted a lifestyle that attached importance to hunting and fishing as modes of subsistence.[23] Some of Sarashina's poems, such as 'Isn't It So?', thus offer glimpses of Ainu helplessly watching dead fish float down the river after spawning. The administrative partition of Hokkaido into agricultural plots for distribution to settlers and Ainu or land declared to be imperial property severely constrained the use of natural resources. The quality of land plots was uneven and corruption sometimes prevented fair land allotment.[24] In Sarashina's poems, Ainu and settlers alike shiver from the cold, unable to procure wood for heating even though pristine forests surround them. And, as poems such as 'Kotan Chronicle' and 'National Census' report, they can only deplore the meagre harvests obtained from the barely cultivable earth they have been given.

The 1899 law, together with a set of regulations enacted in 1901, also confirmed educational segregation. Ainu children had to attend separate schools, or dedicated classes in Japanese schools. The use of their own language was actively discouraged. By 1928, 99 per cent of Ainu children were enrolled in elementary schools, a steep rise from about 18 per cent in 1895. This was a commendable achievement, although in order to promote assimilation, priority was given to Japanese language teaching and explanation of farming methods, rather than the geography, history and science lessons to which Japanese children were entitled.[25] For Sarashina, the system reeked of the traditional Yamato spirit, with its misplaced self-righteousness in subordinating other peoples.[26]

His poems give a voice to Ainu who felt that the 1899 law had trapped them in a vicious circle of dependency and despondency. Most striking is 'As the Old Man Told Me', the first poem of *Seed Potatoes*, which candidly relates the encounter between Japanese settlers and natives. Spoken by a *kotan* elder, the voice is made even more real by the use of hiragana script from start to finish and a blurring of Japanese pronunciation – for example, accentuated consonants and lengthened vowels. In effect, the poetic device, by representing accurately the authenticity of the elder's non-standard speech, acknowledges the distance that exists between the two cultures.

Anger and honesty cut short Sarashina's teaching career. Slightly over a year after starting work in the *kotan* school, he was handed a dismissal letter by the educational authorities. During a Japanese lesson that referred in a text to past Japanese conquests of *emishi*, or 'barbarians', a pupil had inquired about the meaning of the term. Her simple question raised enormous historical issues: does the word refer to the ancestors of the Ainu? Did they really disobey imperial orders as alleged in the text? Did they deserve the punishment of subjugation this implied? The incident, recorded in the poem "The Meaning of "Barbarian"', sparked Sarashina's open questioning of teaching materials and the one-sided historical interpretations they offered. His resistance manifested itself in deviating from the prescribed curriculum, as well as extolling the virtues of Ainu culture and language in his poems. The educational board judged him unfit for teaching because of his subversive ideas.[27] As he explained to a Tokyo anarchist friend, he had become a 'dangerous character'.[28]

But Sarashina had no regrets. He urged his mother not to shed tears on his behalf, as he was not prepared to teach lies and had acted according to his true convictions.[29] For all his compassion and sense of justice, however, he also on occasions showed undisguised irritation at the docile response of the Ainu to the system that denied them freedom and dignity. This is evident in poems such as 'Isn't It So?' and 'Blizzard in the Kotan'. Inspired by the revolutionary literature of the times, these texts deplore the Ainu people's lack of resistance and the weight of superstition that stifled their ability to rebel. Ultimately, however, Sarashina's inclination was more fatalistic than revolutionary. He observed the numbing effect of alcohol on Ainu communities and suggested that that was one factor that had contributed to the loss of their ancestral fighting spirit. Poems composed later in the 1930s, such as 'Lake Mashū' and 'Angry Okhotsk', evoke a sense of defeat in the face of Ainu submissiveness and apparent acceptance of their plight as an 'assimilated' ethnic group.

## LEGACY

The texts collected in this volume were written over a period of a dozen years, before Sarashina left the eastern part of the island. They derive from the experiences of a young man confronting the turbulence of 1930s Hokkaido, still a raw and undeveloped land. As well as poet and farmer, the author was an ethnographer, a member of a settler family and a politically engaged anarchist. The combination of these different perspectives not only enriches the poetry but also offers an interesting analytical lens through which to examine the historical mindset of the period. As the threat of repression mounted and the prevalence of proletarian ideas diminished from the mid-1930s onwards, Sarashina increasingly channelled his energy into the study of Ainu folklore. Having interested himself in Ainu insect lore during his early twenties, he gradually expanded the scope of his studies to Ainu language, music, myths and rituals and other aspects of the culture. The Ainu have no written language, which made the task of recording and retrieving information all the more challenging and valuable.

In 1942, Sarashina published *Kotan seibutsuki*, a three-volume compendium of living things as described by *kotan* Ainu. It marked the start of a long career as a historian and ethnographer of the indigenous people. In 1940, Sarashina had given up life among the forests and lakes of eastern Hokkaido and resettled in Sapporo. His thirty-year old wife Hanako had suddenly died of illness and overwork the previous year, leaving behind two young daughters. In addition, Japan's civilian population was experiencing growing deprivation because of the war and for Sarashina moving to the city meant better chances of making ends meet.

Like many intellectuals of the era, he felt pressured to support Japan's expansionary ambitions abroad; some show of patriotic sentiments increased the likelihood of publication and getting an income. Thus, *Tōgen no uta* (Songs of the Frozen Plain), published in 1943 (but completed a few years earlier), contained a section praising the creation of an East Asian sphere under Japanese leadership. Some of these poems, however, carried double meanings, glorifying but simultaneously grieving for the death of young soldiers at the front.

Sarashina's reputation as a scholar in the field of ethnographic Ainu studies grew after the war, as attested by his voluminous literary production. Amongst other works, he gathered and rewrote Ainu tales, myths and legends from all over Hokkaido. By the time of his death in 1985, he had worked and found recognition as a poet, wood sculptor and draughtsman, as well as a historian and scholar. He had received prizes and become a public figure highly knowledgeable about Ainu traditions. But ironically, the very people who inspired a lifetime of poetry and ethnographic studies, this ethnic group with whom he had shared so much before the war, were never unanimous in acknowledging his work.

Ainu studies remain contentious in present-day Japan. Someone without an insider's introduction finds that even simple inquiries about Ainu life raise suspicion. Feelings of resentment within the indigenous community run deep, relating in part to more than century-old conceptions of the nature of ethnographic and anthropological work. The field of anthropology as a modern science developed in Japan in the latter part of the nineteenth century, and, as in the West, this development happened in conjunction with the acquisition of colonial territories and relied originally on a distinction between advanced and backward races. The internal colony of Hokkaido therefore became a fertile ground for observation of the 'primitive Other'.[30]

Ainu studies offered a space for reflection on the origins, and the civilized status, of the Japanese people. In an early twentieth-century world where conceptions of race and evolutionary theory determined international clout, anthropology offered a supposedly scientific means to assess differentiation between Ainu and Japanese and justify Japan's claimed status as a civilized and enlightened nation.[31] The notion that Ainu people can be objects of study, a practice which occasionally involved the secret removal by anthropologists of human remains from burial sites, is still today a source of distress and indignation within Ainu communities.[32] Likewise, the ready acceptance of the idea that an ethnic group can constitute a 'dying race' sustained research about Ainu culture from its inception. From the point of view of the 'observed', however, the scholarly obsession with gathering and recording cultural forms served to reinforce in the dominant collective imagination the stereotype of a backward people unable to adapt to modernity.[33]

Chiri Yukie (1903–1922), a celebrated native Ainu who transcribed traditional tales into Japanese, expressed astonishment mingled with anger about the vocabulary of 'disappearance' attached to her people. She wrote before her premature death in 1922 that 'nature unchanged from ancient times has faded before we realized it.... [O]ur eyes are filled with anxiety, burning with complaints, too dulled and darkened to discern the way ahead so that we have to rely on others' mercy. A wretched sight. The vanishing – that is our name; what a sad name we bear.'[34]

In those days, the notion of a vanishing race was common in anthropological circles. Sarashina at least partially went along with this in both words and actions. His poem 'Angry Okhotsk', for instance, refers to 'the lingering moan of a perishing people', clearly sanctioning this particular view of history. The ethnographic work he carried out hinted at it too. In 1985, the year of his death, he was involved in a trial related to the unauthorized use in one of his books of photographic material depicting an Ainu girl with a caption referring to a 'people doomed to extinction'.[35]

For supporters of Ainu identity, the social Darwinist discourse of allegedly inevitable extinction represented a denial of their fundamental humanity and an implicit justification of discrimination.[36] Putting Sarashina's poems into context, however, nuances this picture. Although he adopted the rhetoric of the times, a close reading of the texts makes clear that he felt genuine understanding of, and closeness to, the Ainu with whom he lived. To him, their civilization was 'other', but never 'inferior'. His anarchist convictions meant that he rejected the concept of a hierarchy of races as commonly portrayed in the prevailing discourse of the era. Sarashina wrote poetry as an ethnographer who sought to understand the process of cultural encounter that fashioned his world without subscribing to the crude distinction between backward and advanced peoples. He knew the Ainu as a result of sharing with them lived experience in eastern Hokkaido. In his own way, the author of *Kotan Chronicles* showed us what it meant to be human in 1930s' Hokkaido.

NADINE WILLEMS

## NOTES

[1] Michele Mason, *Dominant Narratives of Colonial Hokkaido and Imperial Japan: Envisioning the Periphery and the Modern Nation-State* (New York: Palgrave Macmillan, 2012), 57–59.

[2] Matsunaga Gōichi, *Nihon nōmin shishi* (History of Japanese Farmers' Poetry), vol. 2 (Tokyo: Hōsei Daigaku Shuppankyoku, 1969), 711; Teshikagachōshi Hensan Iinkai, *Teshikagachōshi* (The History of Teshikaga Town) (Teshikaga: Teshikagachō, 1981), 143–44.

[3] *Teshikagachōshi*, 151.

[4] See the introduction to *For Dignity, Justice and Revolution: An Anthology of Japanese Proletarian Literature*, ed. Heather Bowen-Struyk and Norma Field (Chicago: University of Chicago Press, 2016); also Oguma Hideo, *Long, Long Autumn Nights: Selected Poems* 1901–1940, trans. David Goodman (Ann Arbor: Center for Japanese Studies, The University of Michigan, 1989).

[5] Kobayashi Takiji, *The Crab Cannery Ship and Other Novels of Struggle*, trans. Željko Cipriš (Honolulu: University of Hawaii Press, 2013), 17.

[6] See for example in Oguma, *Long, Long Autumn Nights*, 7.

[7] Akiyama Kiyoshi, *Anakizumu bungakushi* (History of Anarchist Literature) in *Akiyama Kiyoshi chosakushū* (Works), vol. 11, (Tokyo: Pal Publishing, 2006), 223-29.

[8] Torii Shōzō, *Kushiro bungaku undōshi – Shōwahen* (History of Kushiro's Literary Movement: Showa Period), *Kushiro sōsho* (Kushiro Monographs), vol. 10, (Kushiro: Kushiroshi, 1969), 46–47.

[9] Richard J. Smethurst, *Agricultural Development and Tenancy Disputes in Japan,* 1870–1940 (Princeton: Princeton University Press, 1986), 95–101; see also Ann Waswo, *Japanese Landlords: The Decline of a Rural Elite* (Berkeley: University of California Press, 1977), 128–29.

[10] Ann B. Irish, *Hokkaido: A History of Ethnic Transition and Development on Japan's Northern Island* (Jefferson: McFarland, 2009), 238–39.

[11] Morikawa Yūsaku, *Genya no naka no Sarashina Genzō* (Sarashina Genzō, Poet of Wilderness) (Sapporo: Teshikagakaikan, 1994), 115.

[12] Ibid., 160–61.

[13] The practice of using *fuseji* lasted until 1941 when it was altogether banned in order to eradicate any sign of protest. See Rachael Hutchinson, introduction to *Negotiating Censorship in Modern Japan*, ed. Rachael Hutchinson (Abingdon: Routledge, 2013), 6–7.

[14] Richard H. Mitchell, *Censorship in Imperial Japan* (Princeton: Princeton University Press, 1983), 196–99.

[15] Akiyama, *Anakizumu bungakushi*, 229; see also Torii, *Kushiro bungaku undōshi*, 45, 118.

[16] See Kusano Shimpei, *Frogs & Others*, trans. Cid Corman and Tamaike Susumu (New York: Grossman, 1969).

[17] Anarchists Ōsugi Sakae (1885-1923) and Shiina Sonoji (1887–1962) were amongst the first translators into Japanese of Fabre's *Souvenirs entomologiques*.

[18] Teshikagachō Kyōiku Iinkai, *Genya kikō* (Travels in the Wilderness), Sarashina Genzō shiryō shōkai (Presentation of Documents about Sarashina Genzō), no. 3, 80 (Teshikaga: Sarashina Genzō Bungakushōnokai, 2013).

[19] Conversation with Sarashina Kō at the Hokkaido Museum of Literature, Sapporo, 16 April 2016.

[20] Matsunaga, *Nihon nōmin shishi,* 718.

[21] Watanabe Shigeru, quoted in Torii Shōzō, *Kushiro bungaku undōshi*, 310.

[22] See Komori Yōichi, 'Rule in the Name of Protection: The Japanese State, the Ainu and the Vocabulary of Colonialism', trans. Michele Mason in *The Asia Pacific Journal: Japan Focus* 11-8, no.2 (Feb. 2013) at http://apjjf.org/2013/11/8/Komori-Yoichi/3903/article.html; Richard Siddle, *Race, Resistance and the Ainu of Japan* (Abingdon: Routledge, 1996).

[23] David Howell, 'Making "Useful Citizens" of Ainu Subjects in

Early Twentieth-Century Japan', *Journal of Asian Studies* 63, no. 1 (Feb. 2004): 7.

[24] Siddle, *Race, Resistance and the Ainu of Japan*, 71; Morikawa, *Genya no naka no Sarashina Genzō*, 114.

[25] Siddle, *Race, Resistance and the Ainu of Japan*, 72.

[26] Watanabe Shigeru in Torii, *Kushiro bungaku undōshi*, 310.

[27] Morikawa Yūsaku, *Genya no naka no Sarashina Genzō*, 128.

[28] Sarashina Genzō, 'Hankyō' (Echoes), *Dinamikku* (1 Dec. 1931), in Ishikawa Sanshirō's *Kojinshi* (self-published leaflets), reprint edition (Tokyo: Kokushokusensensha, 1974), 113.

[29] Sarashina Genzō, *Sarashina genzō shishū* (Collected Poems), ed. Kitsukawa Akio (Tokyo: Doyōbijutsusha, 1986), 32.

[30] Akitoshi Shimizu, 'Colonialism and the Development of Modern Anthropology in Japan', in *Anthropology and Colonialism in Asia and Oceania,* eds. Jan van Bremen and Akitoshi Shimizu (Richmond: Routledge, 1999), 115.

[31] Siddle, Race, *Resistance and the Ainu of Japan*, 76–77.

[32] Mark J. Hudson, ann-elise lewallen and Mark K. Watson, eds., *Beyond Ainu Studies: Changing Academic and Public Perspectives* (Honolulu: University of Hawaii Press, 2014), 3.

[33] See Tessa Morris-Suzuki, 'Tourists, Anthropologists, and Visions of Indigenous Society in Japan', in Hudson et al., eds., *Beyond Ainu Studies*, 45–66.

[34] Chiri Yukie (transliteration and Japanese trans.), 'The Song the God Owl Himself Sang, "Silver Droplets Fall, Fall All Around," An Ainu Tale', English trans. Kyoko Selden, *The Asia Pacific Journal: Japan Focus* 14-15, no.5 (Aug. 2015), 1. On this topic, see also Howell, 'Making "Useful Citizens" of Ainu Subjects', 22.

[35] Chicap Mieko (1948–2010), an artist and writer of Ainu lineage, filed a lawsuit against Sarashina for use of her portrait without permission. The matter was settled with the publishing company after Sarashina's death.

[36] Siddle, *Race, Resistance and the Ainu of Japan*, 76-77.

As always, the process of translation involved choices. Because the linguistic mix of the poems – comprising standard Japanese, Hokkaido and Tohoku dialects, as well as Ainu words – is such a defining feature of Sarashina's work, it seemed important to incorporate some foreign words into the English text. Ainu and Japanese terms, immediately preceded or followed by corresponding English words, are thus printed using different fonts in the translation. This is done the first time such words occur in a poem; on subsequent occasions in the same poem the Ainu or Japanese words appear without the English gloss.

Small capitals in CALIBRI are used for Ainu words which are embedded in the English; italics are used for Japanese words, whether lexical items or onomatopoeia. Italics are also used for direct speech; if a poem – for example, 'Bear Story' – is almost exclusively in italics this marks it as a reported monologue.

The insertion into the poems of words in the Ainu language, which are themselves transliterated into the Japanese hiragana syllabary, also required the selection of a system of transcription into English. Unless otherwise specified in the glossary, the transcription follows John Batchelor's *Ainu English Japanese Dictionary*. This dictionary is less frequently referred to nowadays than Kayano Shigeru's *Ainugo jiten* (Ainu Language Dictionary) but seemed more comprehensive and suitable in this particular case as it contains almost all the Ainu words mentioned by Sarashina, and, in the view of this translator, the transcription makes pronunciation easier for an English-speaking audience. Words that are not found in Batchelor are transcribed according to common usage or alternative dictionary sources.

When words and phrases are truncated or modified in the original to reflect a particular manner of speech, roughly similar linguistic devices are used in English. These modifications to standard English do not in linguistic terms exactly mimic the distortions in the original Japanese; the attempt is rather to give a sense of the cultural complexities that are vital to the poems by providing an English-specific parallel to the stylistic experience of reading the original.

Similar considerations led to the preservation in the translations of most of the original onomatopoeia – called ideophones in linguistics – of which the Japanese language is so fond, as was Sarashina. Such depiction of sounds and properties of the natural world seemed a fitting way to highlight the animism of Ainu culture, a major reference in the poems. Onomatopoeia mimics the magical belief that trees and salmon, mountains and lakes, are indeed spiritual beings who inhabit Hokkaido's vast expanse of land.

Because Sarashina's anti-establishment convictions could incur stiff punishment in his time, some words and phrases were subjected to self-censorship in the original text. Rather than guessing the poet's intentions, such blank spaces are replaced in the translation by '[CENSORED]', which perhaps best attunes today's readers to the harsh literary constraints of pre-war Japan. The notes at the end of the volume include suggestions about possible substitutes.

# from *Seed Potatoes* (1930)

The town of Teshikaga *circa* 1930

*For an explanation of the use of different type-faces in the translations, please see the Translator's Note on page 33. A title marked by an asterisk denotes that there is further information on that poem in the Notes beginning on page 99.*

## AS THE OLD MAN TOLD ME*

*Back in old days when us Ainu*
*Walked barefoot in snow*
*We was strong*
*We didn know our own ages*
*We ate food raw, no boilin no bakin*
*We was niver defeated by none*
*We was strong*

SHAMO *settlers came*
*And Ainu gan to copy* SHAMO *ways*
*And* SHAMO*-masters gan to be bullies*
*Then bellies hurt & feet hurt*
*But when we was young, even sick, even when bellies hurt, we'd run*
*barefoot in mountains*
*We'd walk barefoot even when snow was fallin*

*And we all got along fine*
*Niver any* SHAMO*-like slyness amongst us*
*And we didn tell lies, niver boasted*
*All bad things was taught us by* SHAMO

*Ainu country is real human country*
*And us Ainu, even though us'll all end up dead*
SHAMO *& foreigners'll both die out too*
*Unless the world change to how us see it*

*It's no good boilin & bakin*
*It's good as it is*
*And we'll likely die out for not tellin lies*

*But the gods know everything*
*And if we tell lies, horrible things'll happen*
*Horrible, worse than death*

*D'you see?*
*If your lot mock what I'm sayin*
*Horrible things'll happen    that's no lie*
*We niver tell lies*

# BEAR STORY

*No, you're wrong*
*It's not only bears that are bad*
(The old man who'd been quiet till now
Got up, gestured with his hands as he spoke)

*You see    a bear    it has a life*
*It wants to live    or rather, living's what it does*
*But what do you think    what'll the big fella eat?*
*What is there for him to eat?*
*There's nothing    it's all been taken*
*So they go for the humans who have it    who've stolen it*
*Sometimes you've got to eat humans    even if they don't taste that good*

*Bears    they aren't here for the sole purpose of killing*
*Or being killed by human beings*

*What one big one did    it's an impressive story*
*On my farm*
*It killed eight cows in one night*
*Nothing's ever made me so angry*
*I tracked the bear, I was fully prepared to die*
*Then    there it was*
*The bear had taken a calf away from a cow that had just given birth*
*And was cradling it in its arms in its own den*
*Of course I don't know what the ultimate aim was*

*But anyway as we went in there the bear got startled and fled*
*And then        Yoshimasa you saw it too, didn't you?*
*Didn't the calf cry and follow the bear's tracks –*
*What do you all think about that?*

*As for me, I don't criticise*
*But those know-it-all people*
*What happens is, they force the bear into killing the cows*
*In fact there's plenty of folk whose faces I'd like to see getting*
*walloped by a bear's big paw*

*Right enough        bears are bad*
*But of course anyone could turn out bad*
*If you couldn't eat and were about to die        you'd kill too*
*It's not the bear's fault –*
*But even so I can't live with a bear*

## BLIZZARD IN THE KOTAN*

It's meant to be spring
But a cold wind blasts through the KOTAN
Snow whirls and swirls
And falls without end

Today I think again
About the KOTAN people who live under these skies
Slaughtering bears
Catching salmon in the river
Offering a dark ONGAMI prayer to ABE-KAMUI god of fire
Before the furious flames of a bonfire in the grassland

Dizzy with strong saké these primordial people
Dance, stagger, tire, fall asleep
On waking they mumble a prayer and get drunk again

Sacrificed to ingenuous superstition, to involuntary belief
The fresh blood of a HOKUYUK HEPERE man-eating bear stains
the deep snow
A new INAU totem stands on the hill
Song and dance of an alien, of a tragic custom
Growls and cries of another bear-cub being strangled
And the blood-sullied snow doesn't melt

The KOTAN where these people live
Today again is a blizzard-swept village

Ah! the KOTAN is blizzard-swept
It's meant to be spring
Milk-white light fills the village at the mountain's foot
Yet today the KOTAN where these people live is blizzard-swept
again

## ISN'T IT SO?*

I don't worry about getting fired
If it was money I was after, I'd just keep my head down and not do anything stupid enough to get me sacked

This morning your Kiyokko came and said
– Sensei, *I want to warm myself up by a fire*
There's no firewood though the house is surrounded by forest
– *Ah, I want to eat some fish, the* akiaji *salmon's so good*
Dead *akiaji* float down the river but there are only potatoes to eat
You people descend from those who long ago resisted the [CENSORED]
But all you do is cry yourselves to sleep
The Natives [CENSORED] Law is poison gas
And you wonder what the point of clenching your fist is
Your balls cut off by drinking *shōchū*, your MENOKO daughters stolen
What has this dense bewitching fog done to you?
Isn't it like a *kappa* water spirit coming out onto land
Or a herring taken to a freshwater river?
Don't you understand? How many bear pelts did you trade for those swords that when unsheathed were supposed to bring down divine punishment?
And when you complain, you get called *kusare* rotten Ainu, don't you?
Even I was pretty surprised

The bears aren't fooled
But that's because they don't drink *shōchū*, there's no Protection Law for them
They have the same teeth and claws as always
They go clambering up the mountain
But even Sendo-san no longer sees the point in killing them
*– Bears be pitiful too, naught for they to eat but unripe* sarunashi *picked up crossin the plain yesternoon*

When your *shōchū*'s cut with water you quickly sober up
You get up from near the fire, rub your beard and wonder
What's a [CENSORED], what's a [CENSORED] Law?
What's *shōchū*, what's this bewitchment?
Don't you see how the surveyor's rod has cowed you?
Look! This is how to clench your fist!
It's a lie that the only thing for you to be is *kusare* Ainu

Isn't it so?
Me, I'm quite willing to be sacked
Rise up, you *kusare* Ainu!

On the track sometimes the dog's on top of the child
Sometimes the child's on top of the dog as they play together
The dog *perapera* licks the child's cheeks
The dog rolls the child over, the child's on his back
Above the tip of his nose, he can see the dog's wagging tail
And the blue sky

Black kites are circling
Ever since KOTAN people have been forbidden to catch the
ICHANUI trout
Even if black kites come and wild chrysanthemums bloom
They feel only anger at the kites that eat the spawning trout
All that's left for them is to harvest the oats trampled by the
SHAMO settlers' horses
Even weeds hardly grow now on the land assigned to them
And they lack the strength even to clear those away

HAPO mama went to the fields every day leaving the dog with
the child
So the child had been friends with the dog from the time he
learnt to crawl
When he was tired of playing with the dog, he would take aim
at a *shōchū* bottle
Left empty by ACHA papa and fill it with piss
He grew up, and the dog learnt how to pull a sledge
The child grew skilled *ki ki ki* at making the dog pull the sledge
When tired they fell asleep together in the fields or even on the
path

The child got sick
And after they were told it was serious
For the first time as far as he could remember
HAPO held him in her arms in daylight
And ACHA bought him a caramel sweet
With a weak smile the child decided he liked being sick
Then happy to be feeling like this he died
The caramel he never tasted was put in the coffin
The dog went running *korokoro* to the field
And rubbed its back in the grass

## SCUM TOWN

I don't really have any business there
But at night after work I go to Scum Town
Maybe I ought to keep slaving away like the old blokes in
    bygone days
But now and then I hanker to visit this town that stinks of
    humanity
All kinds of people crammed together jostling and spitting
To get any solace I have to suck the foul air deep into my lungs
I yearn to see the faces of beast-like humans
Dodging under swirls of densely rising dust
Rummaging around trying to get by
It somehow cheers my heart to watch them beating each other
    up so hard that they go blue in the face
Crack, bang, boom, they demolish all falsehood with their fists
People that not even a ragman would touch
Are finer than the rarest plant from the mountainside
Don't whores slice just splendidly through life?
This mass of humans
This sea of humans
This blaze of humans

Mindlessly angry    laughing and chattering
Suffering and making others suffer
Living and dying
In a raw swirl
A swirl that smacks down anyone who tries putting on airs
And never listens to a word they say
And spurns them, telling them to wash their faces and start all
    over again

Their stupid faces stinking of humanity
Gleefully shattering the masks of po-faced hypocrisy
So many of them, grabbing at each other
The swirl spreading, gathering, growing
They say beggars should be blown along by the wind
They say they don't give a damn for anyone else
They say anyone who gets in their way should get knocked flat
They ask how they can get better at lying
A bunch of bastards who look quite capable of cutting others to pieces and roasting them
Brawling and roaring all over the place
In this crowd that spins crazily like a conflagration
If I don't ram head-on into all this enormous energy
I'm in danger of losing my footing
I don't go there to shout abuse at human beings or to flatter them
But because I want to suck the foul air of total human chaos down into my guts
In this place there's no red-horned devil, no lord of the underworld, no god, no Buddha

## THE MAD ENTOMOLOGIST*

*Wait!*
*It's splitting the egg-chamber and coming out now*
*Just thinking about it makes me shiver*
*Could it be the industrious* Chalicodoma?
*Or perhaps one of those parasites?*
*If so will it be a* Stelis *or a* Coelioxys
*Or indeed an enormous* Anthrax *fly?*
*It'd be great to see the face of a* Chalicodoma
*But even if it were the offspring of some ignominious free-rider*
*Never mind, I can hardly wait*

The curtain's about to rise on a year-long epic drama
Sixty-year old Fabre sits without blinking
Watches this strangely noble effort of a birth-chamber being crunched to bits
A peasant woman who thinks he's mad crosses herself
As she passes the shed on the narrow lane

Shaking his grey-haired head he talks to himself
*But these creatures who trick the* Chalicodoma
*Are acting just the same as humans, are just as boundlessly destructive*
*They all live thanks to those who are living    and to those who lived before them*
*It's the merciless law of killing in order to live*

*What is evolutionary theory?*
*Darwin's poodles are making a fuss*
*They say organisms evolved in the past*
*And will evolve in the future*
*But as of now those guys can't come up with any kind of persuasive theory and can only giggle*
*It's unbelievable! – their hypothesis is no more than a whim!*

The June sky is high above him
He sits cross-legged, immobile, muttering
*At my age the one thing I know for sure is that I don't know for sure*

*Even so anyhow, what's this coming out?*
Chalicodoma? Stelis? Coelioxys? Anthrax?
*Or some other weird and wonderful critter?*

## KEI AND POTATOES

These seed potatoes are heavy        it's enough to put my
shoulder out of joint
The larch tree's in bloom, if we don't sow quickly it'll be too
late
Hey, Kei, don't the larch flowers look lonesome?

What's that? You're crying?
Come on, Kei, stop crying
Crying gets you nowhere
Come on, Kei, there's no point in shedding tears
Tears mean silent defeat

Even if the larch tree's lonesome, his flowers bloom quietly
Doesn't it feel good to know he makes sturdy larch-cones better
than anyone?
Guiltless, calmly blooming without scent in a place that
nobody sees
Doesn't he do what he has to do?
Doesn't he get the job done?

Come on, Kei
This year too we'll spread fertilizer again and again
We'll have potato flowers blooming all around
And all those potatoes loafing about in the soil, we'll wake 'em
up
And then *heave-ho, heave-ho*, everywhere you look there'll be
potatoes

## THE SUBSTITUTE TEACHER'S POEM

1

If a kid did it
I'd have to yell at him
But I did it myself

Because nobody was looking
I furtively opened the school's back door
And sprayed pee all over the flowerbed

2

– *Wow!*   *a train!*   *a train!*
– *Children!*   *what's the fuss?*   *look at your books*   *your books*

So I've become a teacher after all

During the next writing lesson all the children wrote
*I saw a train for the first time*

After they'd all gone home
I found myself standing at the window
Watching a train, and the kids shouting – *Look, it's burping*
*black smoke!*

3

– *What would you all like to do?*
– *Go outside and play!*
– *OK. Let's go*
– *Wow. Really?*

– Sensei, *what's this?*
– *A spring gentian whose flowers are the colour of the sky*
– Sensei, *and this?*
– *That's a dandelion bud*
– Sensei, *why does the sun shine?*
– *Because you're lovely kids*
– *Then why does it rain?*
– *Because you're lovely kids*
– Sensei, *why are you alive?*
– *Because you're lovely kids*
– *Then why do you get angry?*
– *Because you're lovely kids*
– Sensei, *why is the world here?*
– *Because you're lovely kids*
– *Why are we alive,* sensei?
– *So that you can all get along*
– Sensei, *who did you learn this from?*
– *From all you lot*

– Sensei, *Tā-chan thumped me*

4

Soon, for not having told you any lies
I may be whisked away from in front of all you lot
Or even before I get taken away, the dark shadow of my heart
May snatch me from the sight of all you lot
But if that doesn't happen, I'll only be here until the new
teacher comes
For six months I'll be the fertilizer of growth for all you lot

But don't worry
Until I plunge forward into pitch-blackness
Until I can no longer even crawl
Until the very last drop of water is squeezed from my brain
I'll place this hand any time on any of your small hands

It's OK, hang on tight
I'll carry you where I'm going
Soon it'll be you who'll have to do the carrying
At that time don't forget
The intrepid arms, shoulders and shouts
That lifted you up from the muddy marsh so you wouldn't
drown

## SMALL FOOTPRINTS

As expected he disappeared into that house
At first there were three sets of footprints
They'd walked arm-in-arm singing songs
Everyone's heels firmly printing the ground
Then there were two and they'd chatted on their way
Leaving their shoeprints in two straight lines along the path
Then there was one and for a while he'd walked straight ahead
Somehow guessing the way without looking down
After he came to a spot with blooming flowers, there were no more footprints on the path
His neat pair of prints met some big prints coming the other way
And stepped two or three paces aside and off the path
Flowers were blooming on the branches of the tree just where they'd stopped
They came out of the woods into a field where they could see the house
And walked straight down a track
Ah!      now I hear a voice from inside reading a book out loud
*Sparrows are coming*
*Crows are coming*

## POVERTY AND AUTUMN RAIN

Whatever you say, if you're poor, I think what you want is
money

The sound of the rain *zokuzoku* shivers my heart

I dread getting ill on top of all this

*Umph!* A load of sodden potatoes on my back as I head back
to my fireless hut

I walk with my heavy load I slither on the squishy slippery
track

I watch my step so I don't fall

Autumn rain sweat tears nose-drips all mixed up

Hungry pigs squeal I throw them potatoes

Chickens still outside and not yet fed

They're silent, motionless, rooted to the spot

Shaking their heads, their crests drooping, sometimes they
seem to be lost in thought

I envy the trees that face the winter naked

But forget that, I have to chop them down for firewood

Right now it's more important to chop wood than feel ashamed
of being someone who people laugh at because he's left-
handed

Chop, chop, split the wood to make a fire

Look, reason's worth less than baked potatoes

That sort of reason people understand merely by reading books
bought with money squeezed out of the likes of us

See, autumn rain's cold for me, cold for everyone

Work, work, work, until I collapse

If I fall down, I'll crawl

My heart's about to burst, but before it bursts, I know what I
have to do

## SALMON

It must swim up-river
There's nothing sadder for a salmon than being caught in a net and salted
No matter what, it's imperative that it swims upstream
The humans know this perfectly well and cast their nets
Then, thankful for the gods' blessing, decorate the dining table with fish-bones

Faced with the imperatives of living
Even creatures smarter than the salmon
Must keep going without reason, even blindly
Those who know this stretch their nets right across the human thoroughfare openly and in broad daylight and what's more in the name of self-preservation
All noble theories have only ever existed in defence of things like this
And people who point this out are labelled traitors and they're [CENSORED]
But however much they're [CENSORED], the truth lives where it lives as long as humans are alive

The indomitable urge isn't caught in the net
A salmon that knows about nets chews them up and rips them    it jumps over them
And by the banks of the flowing snowmelt pouring down from primeval mountain ranges
It deposits millions of new lives deep in the sandy river bed
Only because of this its body has no fear of being transformed into dirt on the river-bottom

## SNOWSTORM

It's a snowstorm
Nobody can see an inch ahead

Having to carry straw sacks on shirtless shoulders in this
weather means that
A piece of firewood makes a handy cudgel which means that
Living people working like the living dead get beaten senseless
which means that
Even though we're hated like demons we go on punishing them
which means that
They're supposed to be grateful just for having a job which
means that
The bottom of a snowdrift is the peaceful graveyard where all
their accounts are settled which means that
If they don't like it there's nothing else for them but to come
up with a story that'll get them arrested and looked after
in jail which means that
They have no choice in the matter –
They understand it clear enough, right?
Don't they understand what's so obvious?

It's a snowstorm, a snowstorm
Nobody knows what's an inch ahead

# Poems from the Early 1930s

Kussharo Kotan Elementary School in 1939

## KOTAN SCHOOL POEMS

### POEM FOR SEKKO

1

For the first time in ages I was eating some *akiaji* salmon I'd
been given when Sekko walked in

– Sensei, *so you don't know much about hard times, then!*
– *There's plenty of this at the spawning grounds where you go, isn't there?*
– *No way!* HAPO *mama brings home only guts and bones and we have to smoke those ready for winter*
– *But if there's enough to smoke that's pretty good, isn't it?*
– *Naah. We have to smoke all of it now if we want to eat in winter*

Fourth-grader Sekko knows what's not in any textbook
The deep-down layers of life

2

*Yesterday we had to run for it*
*Up on the mountain*
*After gathering firewood*
*We heard some bear growls*
*We ran and ran*

*And I saw the little'uns crying on the snow because they couldn't*
*run*
*I had no choice but to grab a stick*
*I thought I'd have to thump the bear if it got too close*
*Sue's father appeared*
*With a dead kite slung across his back*
*'Why are you running away?' he asked, grinning*
*We were so angry at him*
*That I broke the stick in pieces for firewood*
*I won't get fooled like that again today*

3

*Whoosh!*
An apple rolled through a rip in the paper screen behind me
And at the same time – *wa ha ha* – laughter
The sound of small feet running in the corridor

I opened the door and saw
Sekko's eyes laughing at me through a knot-hole in a classroom
wall
– *What are you doing! You keep it!* I said.
– *You eat it,* Sensei – and away she walked, hands folded
behind her

## MAKE-BELIEVE WORK*

There's such a commotion in the playground that I peek out
Yutaka-kachi who came back yesterday from 'going away to
work' is in the centre of things
The kids are yelling *let's pretend we're going away to work!*
Yutaka-kachi is the boss, Yutaka-ji the employee
The two of them do it as they've seen it done on the mountain
Everybody says *let's do the same!*
*– Put your back into it and you'll take home some cash*
On the boss's orders everyone is chanting in rhythm and
making a snowman
*– That's it    I did it    I did!    how much do I get?*
*– You don't get anything    what you get is a punch*
*– What's with that rotten* kusare *boss    wallop him    wallop*
*him*
Yutaka-kachi hunkers down and does a runner
Everyone else in hot pursuit

## CONSTELLATIONS

Evening class is over
*– Right   a good fire lifts the spirit, let's start one*
Sekko opens the bay window to get some wood
*– Wow!   lots of stars*
I see   the starlit sky showing off its gems
*– Look!   that's the North Star   leading the way*
*– And the red one between the trees is Aldebaran*
*– If all those were the* KOTAN*'s cash we could buy anything,*
*imagine that*
*– It's cold   shut the window   a fire's better than stars*
*– OK, let's get the fire going – all star-gazing does for you is give*
*you a stiff neck*

## MAMO'S POEM

1

– *Whoa! Mamo's back!*
– *Oi! Mamo, come here quick!*
– *Ya! Mamo, you're wearing corduroy!*
– *Ooh! He's wearing boots too!*
– *Ya! A new cap! Let me see!*
– *Hoo! Nice and shiny – and a nice peak!*
Whatever they say, Mamo beams
Looks nostalgic, opens and closes the lid of his desk
Everyone gathers round Mamo
– *Mamo, did you go to Bihoro?*
– *How many bags of rice did they give you?*
– *Don't go again!*
– *Mamo's got fat, he's been eating rice!*
– *Mamo's the only one here wearing winter clothes!*
Whatever they say, Mamo just laughs
All day the kids keep glancing his way
They look happy, they smile as they study

2

Taking his cap off or putting it on he took so much care
He grinned and held out its cherished star-shaped badge
– Sensei, *take it*      he blurted
– *Why so?* He went quiet and looked down when I said this
– *I don't need it*
He made a puzzled but happy face

*– Mamo said he was sorry he'd given you all sorts of worries*
*And sorry he came back from Bihoro without a present for you*
*All along he was stroking his cap-badge* – that's what Sekko told me

Mamo is an eleven-year-old youngster, full name Ōya Mamoru

## ATTENDANCE RATE

Since the kids of the migrants who settled across the river
started coming to school
The attendance rate has worsened
*– They shouldn't be lazy, they should be sent out to learn*
I couldn't agree more, so the next day I visited the little house
of the settlers
An old woman alone in a grass shack, the fire had gone out
She was sleeping with her head tied up in a scarf
*– I'd like to send him … but …*
There was nothing to say so I left
On the newly opened-up land at the foot of the still snow-
covered mountain
A small completely dirt-blackened child was carrying burnt
brushwood
I joined in, chopped trees and cleared brush until nightfall

I went home without saying anything about attendance

## THE ABSENTEE

I went to visit the house of a kid who'd been absent for more than a week
The migrants had only recently settled so there was no clear trail to their house
I stumbled into logging roads
I bloodied my foot in a field of bamboo grass
Just as I was turning back unable to find my way no matter what
I suddenly bumped into the kid I'd gone to look for
He was dangling a still moving fish pierced with a bamboo stick
– *What's up?* I asked
– *Okka – it's my mother*   *she's not well*   and he looked down
He was on his way back from catching the evening meal
In the river about a mile from the mountain
– *Look after her then*

– *Sainara* said the kid as he plodded
Back towards the mountain swathed in cloud

## GEOGRAPHICAL OFFENCE

People seek to live where the climate's good for growing things
When I talked about this during the geography lesson
One of the settlers' kids pulled a strange face
That kid came from the Kishū region where the *mikan* oranges grow
He came to this northern island in perfect disregard of geographical laws

## THE MEANING OF 'BARBARIAN'*

– Sensei, *what does* 'emishi' *mean?*
I was shocked when Nanko asked me that as we were reading
*Ototachibana Hime*
*'A life sacrificed in the subjugation of the* emishi ... '
Was clearly written in Nanko's book
Nanko, fingers playing with volume nine of the government-prescribed textbook,
Looked at the cherry blossoms outside the window as she waited for my answer
– *Yes, well* ... I said, but
Instead of an answer innumerable firecrackers jumped out of my eyes

## SUMMER

The lake's warm enough for swimming now
Who cares about end-of-term reports, the summer break starts next week
Cherries are turning black and gooseberries red
Sparrows come to the cherries in the playground, the kids puff out their cheeks
Foot-soles are itching to go

In the classroom when the lesson's over
– *Let's go,* they say, and run barefoot to the lake
They make the raft they've been thinking about in class since morning
They go round the lake    dive in the water
They all line up neatly
Roasting their willies in the sun they shout
– Sensei, *come on in too!*    *loaches*    *let's catch some!*

## GRADUATION CEREMONY

Well, here we are, graduation's tomorrow
And now the time's come I don't like this parting
Until now it's been fine because we shared the burden equally
But from tomorrow it'll be each one for himself
And the load's too heavy for your small shoulders
From tomorrow you'll really be on your own
I wonder how much my few months of effort
Have strengthened the bones of your shoulders
And because the world's nothing like the books of moral
    education
And because you're the ones having to go out there
I wish I could give you all or even half of my strength
But be patient, tomorrow's graduation day
And however far you go, whatever hardship you face
I'll be shoulder-to-shoulder, right there with you
Don't be defeated, amidst this world's raging tides
Be fine, hard-shouldered SEKACHI boys

## NATIONAL CENSUS*

### 1

In the KOTAN they call Takayama Benkichi
*Hanzureoto* (the outsider)

According to the National Census
His job is Welfare Benefit Recipient
But he
Acts big and says
– *They pay me my pension because of my record of meritorious service*
The people of the KOTAN say
– *That may be, but what kind of service is that, cheating us blind*
That's why this fellow's called Hanzureoto

Sixty-nine year old Hanzureoto was born in the fifth year of Meiji
In a shack that looked like a snowstorm would blow it away

### 2

*In short        this Natives Protection Law*
*Is pissing on the Ainu*
*This law        it's meant to shut us up*
*Even if we're cheated        we can't say anything*
*And then we get lazy*
*Without that law*
*Things would have been much better by now*
*It's sad and intolerable*
*The* SHAMO*-masters don't understand*
*Ainu stuff*

*Ainu are human too*
*We're not the* SHAMO*'s pets*
*Me    I want some land*
*If I had some land    I'd work    as best as I could*
*Us    we're not beggars*
*If we don't get it for free    that's fine*
*We want    a place to work*
*We want a job*
*Us    if we don't work*
*We don't earn anything –*
*And that's why I've gone completely bald*
And the KEMASHITEPU old man burst out laughing

3

Only one man from the KOTAN went to the front for the Russo-Japanese War
People say he has the Sixth Order of Merit

*When we got to the front, what surprised us most*
*Was a soldier lying on his back and humming away to himself*
*Under a swarm of flying bullets*
*And, seeing our faces, he said*
*'Ahah! More bullet fodder's arrived!'*
*That pissed us off*
*And every day after that we were thinking*
*'Are we going to die today?    Or will tomorrow be the day?'*
*When evening came, we thought we'd made it through one more day*

*The old soldiers wouldn't move, saying life was worth more than military discipline*
*The commander would show his power by giving pointless orders from a safe place*
*Us, we weren't worth much, we were supposed to exhibit ourselves as brave living targets*
*To threaten the enemy*
*You've got to be kidding!*
*Shown such a mountain of corpses, such a river of blood*
*Any honest person would flee*
*Honour would be no use whatsoever*
*But then what?*
*Us returning alive and the commander dead at the front?*
*That'd be strange either way*
*So once back home I immediately put that medal into pawn*
*I drank and drank   well, I drank to my heart's content*
*The official certificate's still at the pawn shop, you know*
*It's weird for me to get a medal*
*Properly speaking, military jail would've been more like it*
*When I was crossing the Yalu River, I fell into the water because I wasn't looking where I was going*
*Well, it just happened   it can't be helped*
*I was splashing my way across the river*
*And then the commander shouted from behind*
*'Follow Lance-Corporal Hasegawa!'*
*At first I didn't understand what it was about*
*But the commander seemed to think that I'd jumped into the river*
*Because somehow crossing the bridge was too slow*
*That's the Yamato spirit!*
*Guns only shoot noise*

*But nobody could possibly bayonet a man*
*If there are people who can do that they'd kill a man anywhere*
*Only the kind of person who'd get a medal would find that easy*
*You know you get treated cruelly as a prisoner too*
*Two or three people, and the procedure gets cumbersome*
*So we'd just dispose of them half-way through*
*These are the only things that stay in my mind now*
*Not a single act of bravery*
*Everything's a lie*
*Who's got something more precious than life?*
*If you say something like that*
*They'll say to you, 'Come over here, I'll show you!'*
*It's true*

4

The blind KORUHUCHI old woman
Has a daughter whose children are all by different fathers
Taking her two older children with her the daughter
Goes away to work on a farm in Bihoro
The old woman stays at home with three grandchildren

As for the old woman's age, she was still a child in the year of
 the big landslide
Her name is Sharikin
Whether she has a Japanese name as well I don't know
She's always holding a pair of ABE-BASHUI fire-tongs
When her grandchildren mess about with the fire while
 roasting *tōkimi* corn

ABE-HUCHI – *Old Lady Fire!* she shouts *How many times do I have to tell you?*
She bangs on the hearth frame and tells them off
The children make faces from a safe distance
And flee barefoot from the house

I checked at the town hall but
Didn't find a Japanese name, only Sharikin
Nor did I find in which year the landslide happened
The old woman, rather than talking about this
Was saying she simply couldn't wait
To eat the rice that would come from Bihoro

5

Pa, a SHAMO, born in the fourth year of Bunka, was older than Ma's own dad
Ma, born in the fifth year of Meiji, was the last of six children
When her brothers were old enough they'd all gone away
Her sisters, like her, married SHAMO, and although they lived in the KOTAN
They hardly ever visited

In the house were Pa and Ma
And sixth-grade Take, and Yoshi, the last child
Pa, even at eighty, went out to the fields and cut wood
He said it was because he was of samurai stock
But it seems there was another reason

Pa was hard of hearing
And from the house with broken windows
We could hear loud voices as if arguing

6

There was a commotion in the house next door so she dropped by
They said that HAPO mama was dying
Everyone was gathered round HAPO who had turned blue
They were cooling her with water and massaging her body

HAPO at last regained consciousness but said nothing
Wiping away the folk medicine that stuck around her mouth
Holding back her tears, she looked down
*Ah listen* her elder daughter said
*Why is* HAPO *a* MENOKO *Ainu woman?*
*Because if* HAPO *is* MENOKO
*I have to be* MENOKO *too*
HAPO kicked her away

Kisekko, about to turn six, standing on hoarfrost
Secretly told me this

7

Shige's looking after the child
Mamo's training to carry a box of *mikan* oranges on his back

Matsu, back from the bunkhouse, has a swelling belly
Kimiko, who doesn't know anything, is playing with frog's eggs
she scooped out of the pond
In the laurel patch by the lakeside a *dedeppoppo* turtledove is
calling
The buds the crows eat have completely opened
Here and there oats are seeding
The rooster bristles its wings and runs after the hen
Mother's thoroughly agitated
Even if you feed five kids only with potatoes it's still hard
Even if Father's different every night is there any need for
blame?
In the water in front of the house frogs *kerokero* croak

Shige's house looks as if it's crowned with a bamboo basket
Tonight, too, light from its wood-fire seeps out like a halo

8

*– Flowers don't bloom much here*
*And there isn't much birdsong either*
*When will spring come?*     *It's so cold*
*There's not much here except snow*
*The soil seems worse than at the farm next door*

Hanako, who'd just come as my bride, had some sharp words
to say
My answer was simple:

*– It's because this is Natives Protection land*

Even though in the past all land was free for everyone
Now, even land that's worse than grazing for cows
If you don't cultivate it, they take it away

ACHA papa and HAPO mama were talking in the field
*– What would be good to grow        on that cracked soil?*
*– But seriously, is summer coming?*
*Snow's falling even though it's time for sports day*
*– Sports day might come but we can't do anything*
*– It's fine if summer doesn't come        as long as there's money*
*and rice*

*– When hard times hit how far*
*Will our money go?* he said
*Actually, it'd be easier to be dead*
*That way there'd be no worry about money*
And at that he gave a feeble laugh

## LEAVING THE KOTAN

I

When I entered the classroom some pupils were already
hanging their heads
I got onto the podium, but I didn't know what to say either
As I tried to speak I felt the dam of my eyelids about to give
way
Yesterday evening the headmaster dropped by
*This came,* he said, and handed me a piece of paper
On it was written: *Dismissal of Substitute Teacher*

*I couldn't tell lies*
*I have to leave you*
*Take care of yourselves and study hard*
*Become fine people*
*Make a fine* KOTAN

These things I said in bits and pieces
My words broken up
By the children's tears

*Sayonara*

I ran out of the classroom and out to the back of the building
The flower bed we'd been tending since spring
Wasn't yet in bloom
I thought: come autumn, cosmos and zinnia
And even rose moss
For sure would embellish the KOTAN

2

The girls were making kimono for their dolls with fabric
    Hanako had given them
They'd stopped crying
The boys were looking at an old magazine of mine
– Sensei, *you can have this*
Said Sekko, secretly giving me the exercise book
With a composition I'd recently praised her for
And Kisseko gave a penny candy to Hanako
Unable to bear any more we slipped away into the shadows

3

Once I'd packed my few belongings
The room became a void
I laid out a last meal on the scuffed table
We baked the trout that the EKASHI old man had brought us
And we ate our melancholy supper
Hanako vigorously polished the chimney of the lamp
Igari-kun played a farewell song on the violin

I opened the window and the moon was hazy
Over there in the KOTAN children
Were singing the song 'Rainy Uncle Moon'

4

I'd just finished packing when it started raining
*– It'll rain tomorrow, let it come thrashing down*
*Tomorrow and the day after, for five days, for ten days*
The children in the gym poked their heads out of the window
*– It'll be good if it rains so our teachers won't have to go …*
Even children who'd just been crying went out
Looking up at the sky and wishing

*– Rain, rain, please rain*
They all gathered and played noisily far into the night
Even when worried parents came to check, they wouldn't go home
They said they'd give teacher a send-off at his house the next day
But before they knew it they were making sweet sleep-noises
And above the sleepless roof
It seemed as if it would rain forever
Harder and harder came the rain

5

I said goodbye, bowing, failing to find any words
Everyone took a break from working in the fields
They saw me off, not saying a word, at the outskirts of the KOTAN
The blind EKASHI old man and KORUHUCHI old woman
Stood in front of their house, hands together in gratitude

At the bridge across the Kushiro River
I took the children's hands to say a last farewell
The children were silent
They followed me every step, every step of the way

It was more than a mile from the KOTAN to Noboriondo
We drank water from the stream there and talked for a while
I told them strictly not to come any further
The children waved until I came to a bend in the road and they
disappeared from view
Even though I could no longer see them the sound of *sainara*
Has followed me ever since, ever since

## from *Songs of the Frozen Plain* (1943)

Lake Mashū

## FOREST

The forest wakes from a world of long endurance
The trees stretch     tap each other's shoulders
Rub their hands together still a little chilled by the light wind
All kinds of trees gather and mingle
More and more humble, more and more gentle, they surge upwards
Without blending in without losing individuality
They chat *zawazawa* about the past winter
They hug, they grieve for a friend who fell in pain
Then quickly before anywhere else
Earthly stars scatter the yellow or white joys of life
And every morning a layer of fine green silk is hung over the tree-tops
*Chichichichi*     small birds arrive
That southern song begins
The forest
Doesn't know what intellect or logic is
Thickening gradually     green piles up
Now in a flash the dream becomes a breathing reality
Here and there are bright-eyed marshy places
Where small birds and wild animals come to drink
Beyond that is the immense deep black forest
What does the silent undergrowth make of this spilling sunlight?
And what are these tree shadows where the deep greenery secludes itself
These shadows that nowhere in this heavy thicket show any sign of affectation?

Deep contemplation and admiration for resilient thinking
inhabit the forest
The children for whom this place is home walk back from
school
Every day singing as they go
And a soft evening glow
Always appears from behind the mountain
A vast hush once again quietens the whispering forest's heart
In the bosom of the forest where faint rays of light linger
A fox family unexpectedly emerge
No wild animal's cunning, no suspicion, no animosity
*Kasakasa* grass-blades make a slight sound
An owl cries
Startled, the foxes run back into their den
The light gradually fades
Before long a seasonal moon rises above the slumber

The ochre song that comes from northern seas sweeps across
the uplands
The boundless white harvest gods come
The forest vaunts its glorious demise becomes radiant
The seasons turn the pages of a strict and lofty philosophy
Young branches busily flutter their hands to shed dead leaves
And so the trees
Reveal their true shapes
To the world of constraints once again

Ezo mountain birds blow a frozen flute
Squirrels swing from branch to branch dislodging snow
Everything is white      everything is harsh
Let it come
Even if what's coming from the greyness over there
Is the torment of a predestined snowstorm
Even if it's the solemn ice coating the trees
That greets the distant sun on the white frozen hills
The forest now      by no means dreams of the faraway summer
It only believes in its roots anchored strongly in reality
It tests the flexibility of eternal youth
And so it becomes mighty
And spring returns eternally

## LAKE MASHŪ*

The lake has become a mist-covered sea
Coppery mugwort
Blankets the Kushiro plain, the farthest edge of the grazing
    fields
What's that passing by?
A troop of horses? Cloud shadows?
A dark wandering tribe?

Eyes closed in the fog of meditation
What is the angry KAMUI owl-god thinking?
The hunters' fires burnt out
The mountain ash not blooming red

When the mist clears the lake is a cold eternal blue
The blood and tears of angry gods – have they turned to
    stones?
The great mother of these people – exhausted, has she become
    an island?
Her pure soul – what became of that?

White clouds tower for thousands of years
Solitude is polished by the blizzards
A mountain, and then another, in the end becoming sky
While
The immeasurable wind blows across the apex of heaven

## ANGRY OKHOTSK*

Is it the cry of the darkening sky
Or the lingering moan of a perishing people?
Wind of Okhotsk
Giant birds of the MOSHIRPA east still beat their wings
What's a race?        What's a tribe?

Is it only the howling wind that angers the sea
The sea that bares its fangs, bent on erasing all traces of shame
        and injustice,
Committed to washing away a brutal history?
Sea of Okhotsk
Stone tools destroyed, bones decaying
At Mount Fate the orange lilies are in disarray

Fierce wind and rain recite the faraway SAKORPE epic
Of a defeated OTTENA chief asleep in his KASHI shelter in the
        dark forest
They tell of love in the cave dwellings, of the roses flowering
        red
What elegy is sung by the drenched sea birds
Over the angry Sea of Okhotsk?

## CRANES

The snow-cloud's pure whiteness falls and settles
Becomes a still, enduring presence

No webbed feet to swim with time's current
No pusillanimous wings that chase the seasons
SARORUN KAMUI crane gods of the marshes
Conscientiously starving, they die on the icy plain
Even in the middle of a snowstorm not once do they dream of
going south

Cranes of the sky
This is heretical
How about ideals? What about justice?
Now the land is low and dark and cold
Now's the time to let the sacred fire burn
To let the heart be consumed by immaculate white peace
Look
Cranes fly over the subarctic zone

## THE GREY HERON

Winter sunlight touches the Ezo hazels
A blue shadow stretches on the frozen plain
A grey heron lifts one leg
Quietly closes its eyes and listens to the wind
The wind pushes against the reeds
And moves on elsewhere

The feathers around its ears quiver slightly
It hears something on the desolate heights
Is it the season of despair making its breast feathers tremble?
Or the sound of water flowing deep in the icy river?
Or the yearning for the blue sky throbbing in its heart?

Winds pass through
Seasons shift
But the grey heron doesn't move
Until from its innermost depths its soul takes flight
Emaciated, shaved away by the wind
It becomes unforgiving dry bones
A frozen blue shadow
Not moving

## KUCCHARO KOTAN*

The willow tree's blessing    at the marsh's edge
And in the peaceful hometown
And on the mountain where the KAMUI gods live    and in the water
And the black lilies' love in the forest shade
But sight's gone now    impossible to see the dim rays of spring

In the south they fought and lost
Pure hearts    they embraced the fire, they crossed the ocean
They built their hometown on icy land
The grasses of the KAMUI KOTAN are windswept
Clouds are angry and lash the plain
From where in the twilight do they come pouring?
Autumn is mute
CHEP KAMUI god of fishing    is old now
White noise across mountain peaks
CHUP KAMUI god of the moon    what's he thinking, what's he saying?

Mountain    sharp shrill coughing fit
KUNNE REK KAMUI night-crying owl-god    his voice cracked
What's he saying now?
He rests his head against the god of lingering fire
He hears the sound of winter hooves galloping across the frozen plain

# Notes on the Poems

## NOTES ON THE POEMS

AS THE OLD MAN TOLD ME The old man was Teshi Kanji (1865–1940), also referred to as Kamuima, a blind Ainu elder from Kussharo Kotan. Sarashina met him while working as a teacher in the Kotan primary school and learnt much from him about Ainu myths and customs. Apart from its title, the poem is written in hiragana script, the Japanese phonetic syllabary. The translation uses English-specific distortions to convey the old man's idiosyncratic manner of speech and how much it differed from standard Japanese pronunciation and intonation.

BLIZZARD IN THE KOTAN *Iomande*, the ritual sacrifice of a bear cub, is an essential and well-known ceremony in Ainu culture. It used to take place early in the year, when snow was heavy on the ground. Preparation for the ceremony involved the fabrication of traditional totems, the *inau*, and praying to Abe-kamui, the fire goddess, to secure her blessing. Dancing, singing and story telling also preceded the actual killing of the bear.

ISN'T IT SO? In the spirit of the proletarian politics of the period, the text exhorts the Ainu to rise up against their Japanese masters. It is also an indictment of the Former Natives Protection Law, of 1899, which, despite its name and intentions, contributed to the persistence of discrimination against the Ainu. It seems likely that in the self-censored phrase, 'the Natives [CENSORED] Law', the original word 'Protection' would have been replaced by 'Oppression'. The other censored word probably referred to the emperor or emperors of Japan. It is thought that Ainu resistance to imperial rule was particularly significant between the seventh and tenth centuries (see line 8). In 1869 the Ainu were made subjects of the emperor by fiat, which would justifiably make them wonder what an emperor was (penultimate stanza).

In the third stanza, Sarashina hints at the credulity of the Ainu because they paid too high a price (in bear pelts) for swords, which they traditionally procured from the Japanese. The 'divine punishment' probably alludes to an Ainu legend called *ipetam*, literally 'eating sword'. Although the particulars vary from one region to another, it usually involves a magic sword that has the ability to sense the presence of an intruder around the *kotan* and make a distinctive warning noise. In one version of the story, the sword would then unsheathe itself, kill the enemy, and return to its sheath on its own. It seems that the Ainu strongly believed in the magical power of some swords.

THE MAD ENTOMOLOGIST The work of French entomologist Jean-Henri Fabre (1823-1915) was popular among early twentieth-century Japanese radicals, particularly anarchists. They were familiar with the Frenchman's detailed depiction of the life of mason bees, or *Chalicodoma*. The bees are known for their habit of constructing a hard, dome-like nest with mud and other materials, in which they deposit their eggs. Fabre vividly describes how parasites, such as the *Stelis* and the *Anthrax* fly, introduce their own eggs into the nest, where they develop and begin eating the larvae of the *Chalicodoma*. As the poem suggests, when the time arrives for breaking the dome's shell and leaving the nest, the insect that comes out may not be the offspring of the *Chalicodoma*.

Nineteen-century European anarchism stressed the importance of drawing lessons from the natural world in order to reflect on the management of human affairs. Japanese anarchists' interest in the work of Jean-Henri Fabre was in part motivated by their willingness to find in science some templates of organization for the social sphere. In their view, entomology opened a window into nature's complexity. It highlighted the existence of an intricate web of life, which was characterised by mutual dependency between organisms and could not solely be explained by the crude law of the survival of the fittest.

Fabre was a staunch critic of Darwin's theory of evolution. In his account, only God's grand design could explain the apparent perfection of nature's work. He saw Darwinism as a fad of the times, whose practitioners were overly keen on objectivizing mechanisms of change while neglecting the creative instinct of organisms. Japanese anarchists' endorsement of Fabre was a way of criticising that aspect of evolutionism, even though they were sceptical of religious explanations. Rather, they saw Fabre's descriptions of the insect world as an antidote to what they considered as the scientific reductionism and specialism that guided Japan's modern development.

MAKE-BELIEVE WORK The aggressive development of Hokkaido from the Meiji period onward entailed among other things deforestation and the employment of migrants and Ainu by logging companies.

THE MEANING OF 'BARBARIAN' The term *emishi*, translated here as 'barbarian', originally refers to the people of north-eastern Japan (now the Tōhoku region) who fell outside the imperial polity, including, it is thought, the Ainu people. Over the course of the eighth and ninth centuries, Japanese rulers consolidated their control and the *emishi* were either assimilated into local communities or pushed further north. *Emishi* resistance, however, sporadically re-emerged for a long time afterwards.

Princess Oto-tachibana was the wife of Yamato Takeru (*c.* 72–114), the prince sent to subdue the *emishi* who had allegedly disobeyed imperial wishes. Japanese legend states that she threw herself into the sea during a storm in order to appease the sea god and ensure safe passage of her husband's forces.

NATIONAL CENSUS The fifth year of Meiji was 1872; the fourth year of Bunka, 1807 – although this second date appears to be a mistake on Sarashina's part as it would make Pa (in part 5) more than 120 years old at the time of the poem. It seems likely that, rather than Bunka (文化), Sarashina meant the fourth year of Kōka (弘化), that is 1847, which would have Pa about eighty years old at the time of writing, as the poem states.

LAKE MASHŪ The water of Lake Mashū is some of the clearest in the world, but the lake itself is often shrouded in mist or heavy fog, hence its reputation for mystery. It has inspired Ainu myths as a site inhabited by the gods. In Ainu culture, the *kamui* owl-god, cited in the poem, is an important deity who is guardian of the land and oversees the proper conduct of rituals by humans. Sarashina also refers to the legend of an old woman who became an island, a story he heard from the 'old man' Teshi Kanji (see the note above on the poem 'As the Old Man Told Me') and retold as follows:

*'The small island in the middle of Lake Mashū, that looks like a black-clad puppet master, still now is called Kamui-Shutsu. Kamui-Shutsu refers to a spirit-like old woman who was the mother of a powerful village chief in the north, near Wakkanai. One day almost the whole of the chief's family was ambushed and killed by a neighbouring clan. The old woman, however, managed to rescue the chief's only son, taking him away from the hands of the enemy and fleeing under cover of darkness. But as she was wandering through fields and mountains, she became separated from the grandchild whose life was dearer to her than her own.*

*Full of grief and desperately searching for the lost child, the tired old woman arrived one day at the shore of Lake Kussharo and asked the gods of the lake for shelter for the night, but for some reason they failed to answer. She thus had no choice but to start again and keep walking until she got to Lake Mashū. There, since Mount Kamui happily gave her shelter, she decided to rest in the middle of the lake and ended up becoming an island.*

*And still these days, when people go to the island, the old woman sheds tears of joy at the thought that her grandchild is paying her a visit. It is said that this is why even on days which are clear elsewhere, at Lake Mashū rains falls in summer and it snows in winter.'*

ANGRY OKHOTSK Shakushain's War of 1669 marked the last major attempt by the Ainu to assert their independence from dominance by the Yamato (Japanese) people, particularly with regard to terms of trade. *Ottena* (chief) Shakushain united Ainu clans previously in conflict and led a campaign against Japanese intrusion into their lands. His forces were defeated at the end of 1669, but a sense of betrayal long remained as Japanese warriors treacherously assassinated him and other Ainu combatants after surrender and the negotiation of a peace settlement. For Sarashina, the Okhotsk Sea expresses anger at this act of betrayal.

KUCCHARO KOTAN Kuccharo and Kussharo are the same place. Kuccharo is the name originally given to the *kotan* by Ainu people, but when the Japanese adopted this appellation, they changed the pronunciation to Kussharo. Thus, the official (government) name for the school where Sarashina taught (see the picture on page 62) was Kussharo Kotan Elementary School.

## GLOSSARY (AINU)

From John Batchelor, *An Ainu-English-Japanese Dictionary* (Tokyo: Iwanami Shoten, 1981 [1938]). Words not found in Batchelor are transcribed according to common usage or alternative dictionary sources and are marked with an asterisk.

| | |
|---|---|
| Abe-bashui | fire-tongs |
| Abe-kamui | the goddess of fire (*also* Kamui-huchi) |
| Acha | father, uncle |
| Ainu Moshir(i) | Ainu-land |
| Chep | fish |
| Chup | the sun, moon |
| Chup-kamui | (god of) the sun or moon |
| Ekashi | an ancient, grandfather |
| Hapo | mother (*also* abo, habo) |
| Hepere | a cub |
| Hokuyuk | a man eater |
| Ichanui | sea trout |
| Inau *or* inao | a shaved wooden wand, totem |
| Iomande | to send away, to sacrifice |
| Kamui | a god |
| Kashi | a lodge |
| Kemashitepu* | an old man |
| Koruhuchi* | an old woman (*also* korohuchi) |
| Kotan | a village |
| Kunne | dark, night |
| Menoko | a woman |
| Moshir(i)pa | the east |
| Ongami | to adore, adoration, prayer |
| Ottena | the chief of a village |
| Rek | to sing, to cry |
| Sakor(o)pe* | an epic, a legend |

| | |
|---|---|
| Sarorun | a crane |
| Sekachi | a boy |
| Shamo | a Japanese (*also* shisam) |

## GLOSSARY (JAPANESE)

Any italicised Japanese words not included in this glossary are onomatopoeic.

| | |
|---|---|
| Akiaji | salmon (especially salmon swimming upstream in the autumn), salted salmon |
| Emishi | (see the note on page 101) |
| Ezo | historical name for the lands north of the main Japanese island of Honshu |
| Kappa | a water imp |
| Kusare | rotten, worthless |
| Mikan | mandarin orange |
| Sarunashi | hardy kiwifruit |
| Sensei | teacher, master |
| Shōchū | clear liquor distilled from potatoes, rice, buckwheat, etc. |

*Dialectal pronunciations:*

Hanzureoto = *hazure no otoko* = man at the edge, outsider
Okka = *okāsan* = mother
Sainara = *sayonara* = goodbye
Tōkimi = *tōmorokoshi* = corn

Lightning Source UK Ltd.
Milton Keynes UK
UKOW04f2300290817
308194UK00001B/23/P

9 784907 359195